Cut & Fold
EXTRATERRESTRIAL INVADERS
That Fly
22 FULL-COLOR SPACESHIPS

Michael Grater

Dover Publications, Inc.
New York

INSTRUCTIONS

These extraterrestrial invaders are easy to make and they really do fly. The only tools you will need are

scissors
transparent tape
cardboard
paper clips
ruler or other straightedge

Begin by cutting out one of the invaders, following the heavy black outline as carefully as you can.

Next, protect your work table by covering it with a piece of cardboard. Lay the cutout on the cardboard and score along the fold lines (single or double dashed lines). Single dashed lines tell you to fold *back*, so that the lines remain visible to you. Double dashed lines tell you to fold *forward* so that the lines get hidden in the fold. (See Figure A.)

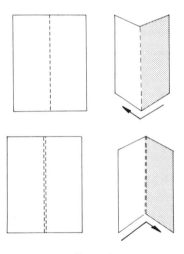

Figure A

Score single lines by laying a ruler next to them and drawing a scissors point along the whole length; apply some pressure, but not so much as to cut through the paper. Score double dashed lines *halfway* between the two.

After you've scored all the fold lines, fold them in sequence, following the order of the circled numbers. As you do this, refer to the explanatory diagrams that show you step-by-step how each invader is made, including when and how the tail plane is raised above the fuselage in some models. (See Figure B.) Note that to achieve the proper symmetry, the same folds are made on both wings. It is essential that all folds be made crisply and exactly where indicated.

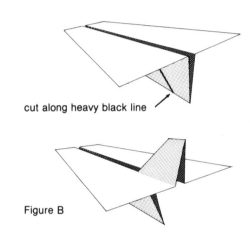

cut along heavy black line

Figure B

Before flying the invader, give the nose a little extra weight by adding a paper clip. You may also want to secure folds with little pieces of transparent tape at the top of the body and at the front of the tail. (See Figure C.)

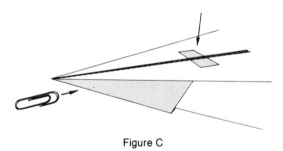

Figure C

Test-fly the invader, increasing or decreasing the angle where the wings meet the fuselage until you find the dihedral that works best. If the invader corkscrews or spins when launched, the configuration of the wings is irregular because some of the folds have not been done precisely right. Correct this by unfolding and refolding more carefully.

EXPLANATORY DIAGRAMS FOLLOW PLATES

Copyright © 1983 by Michael Grater.
All rights reserved under Pan American and International Copyright Conventions.

Published in Canada by General Publishing Company, Ltd., 30 Lesmill Road, Don Mills, Toronto, Ontario.
Published in the United Kingdom by Constable and Company, Ltd.

Cut & Fold Extraterrestrial Invaders That Fly is a new work, first published by Dover Publications, Inc., in 1983.

International Standard Book Number: 0-486-24478-4

Manufactured in the United States of America
Dover Publications, Inc., 180 Varick Street, New York, N.Y. 10014

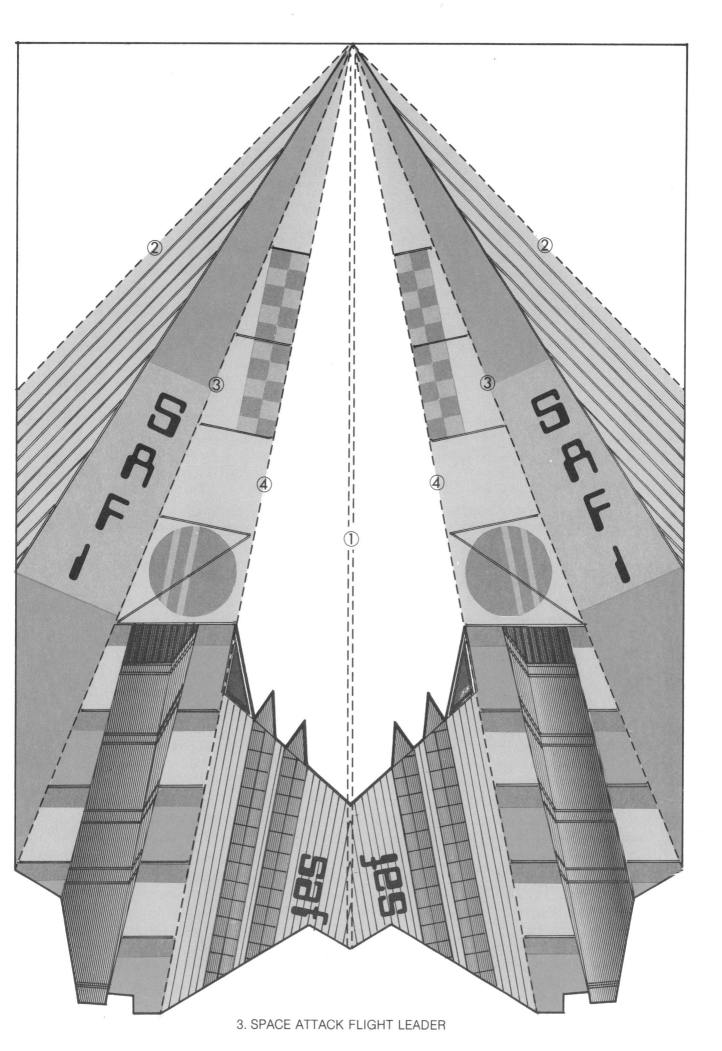

3. SPACE ATTACK FLIGHT LEADER

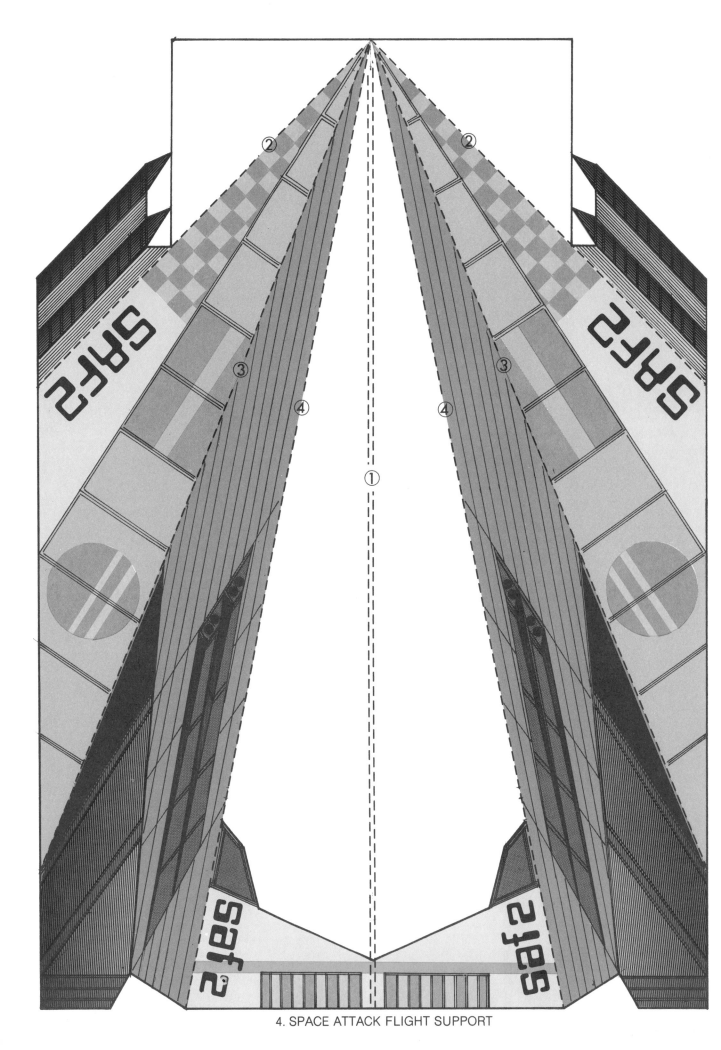

4. SPACE ATTACK FLIGHT SUPPORT

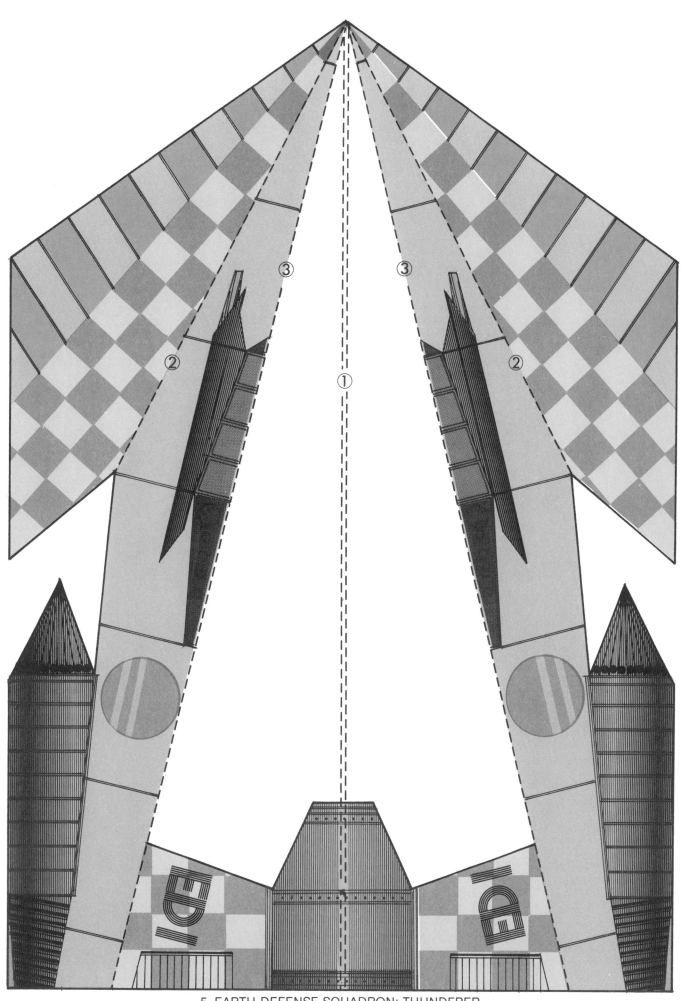

5. EARTH DEFENSE SQUADRON: THUNDERER

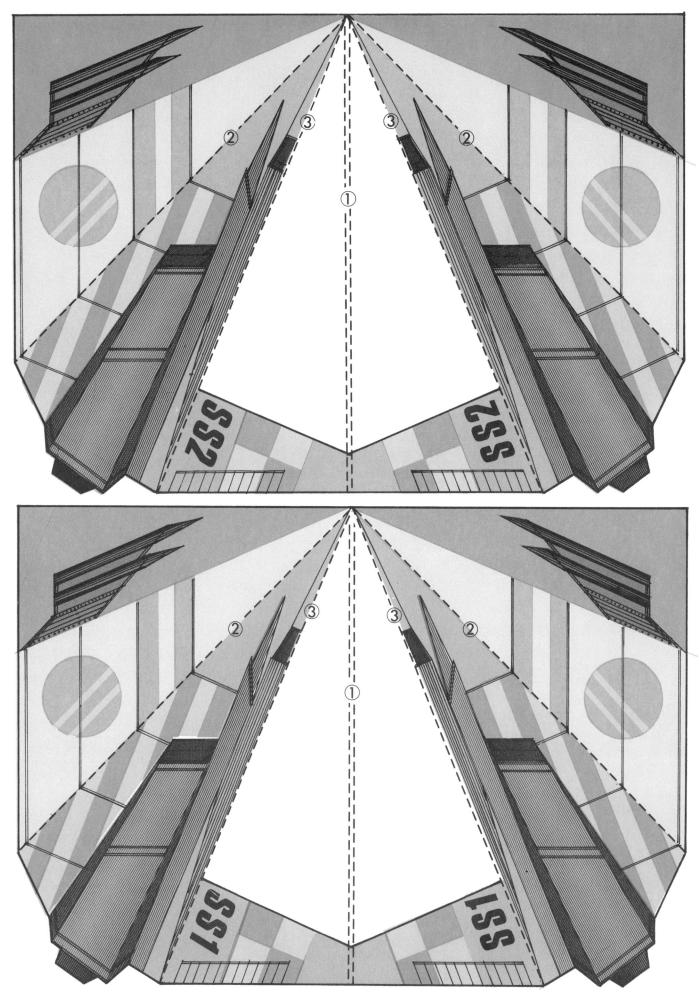

6. SPACE SCOUT and SPACE SCOUT SUPPORT (2 fliers)

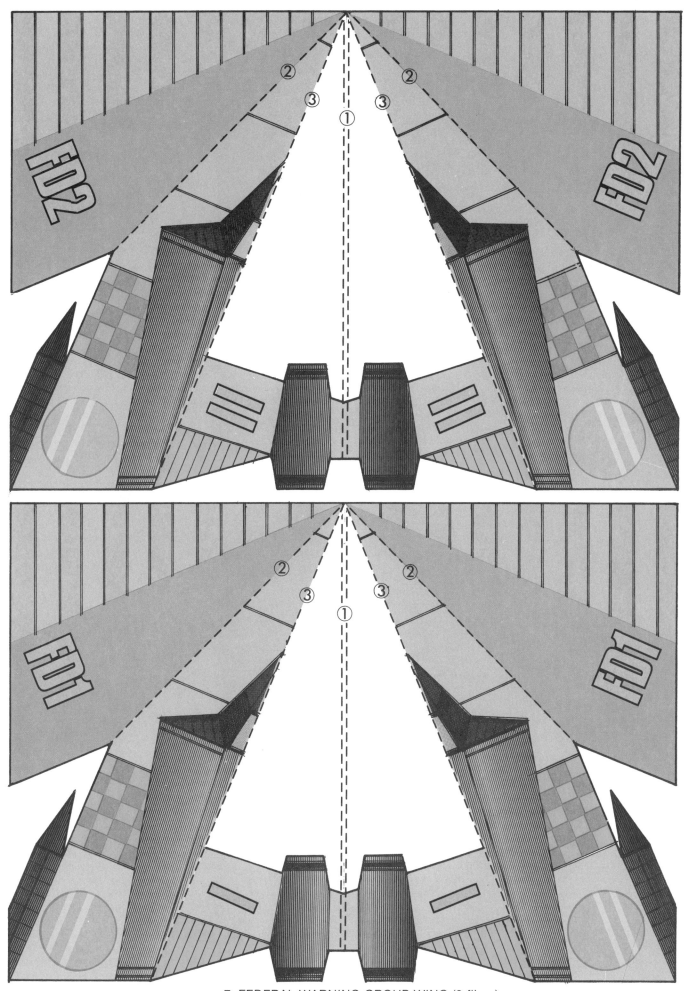

7. FEDERAL WARNING GROUP WING (2 fliers)

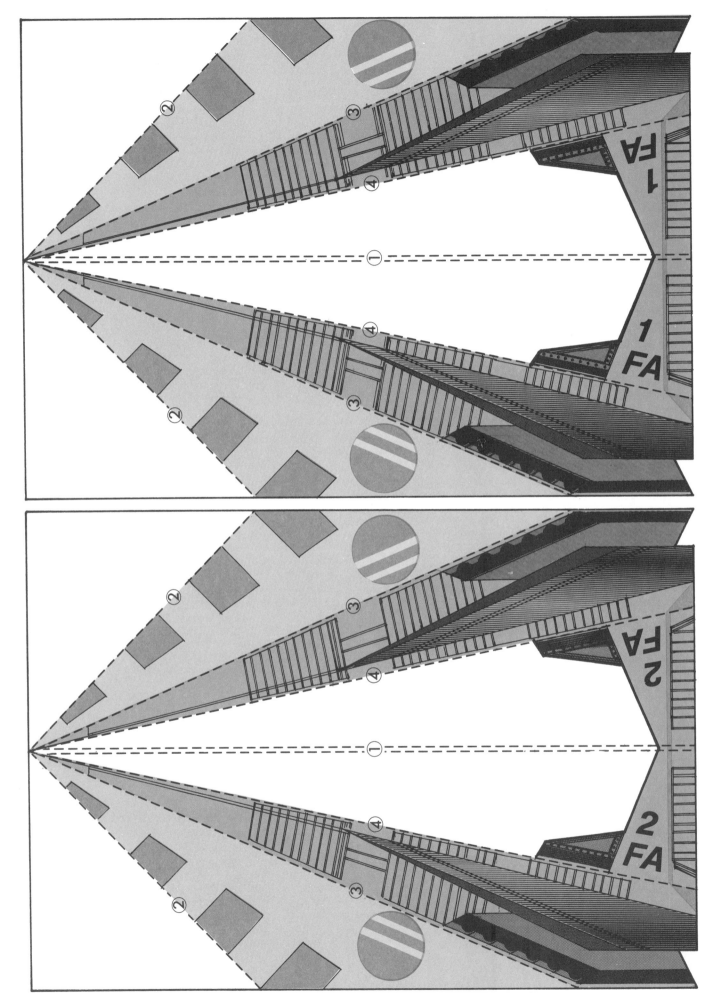

8. FEDERAL ALERT FLIGHT LEADER and SUPPORT (2 fliers)

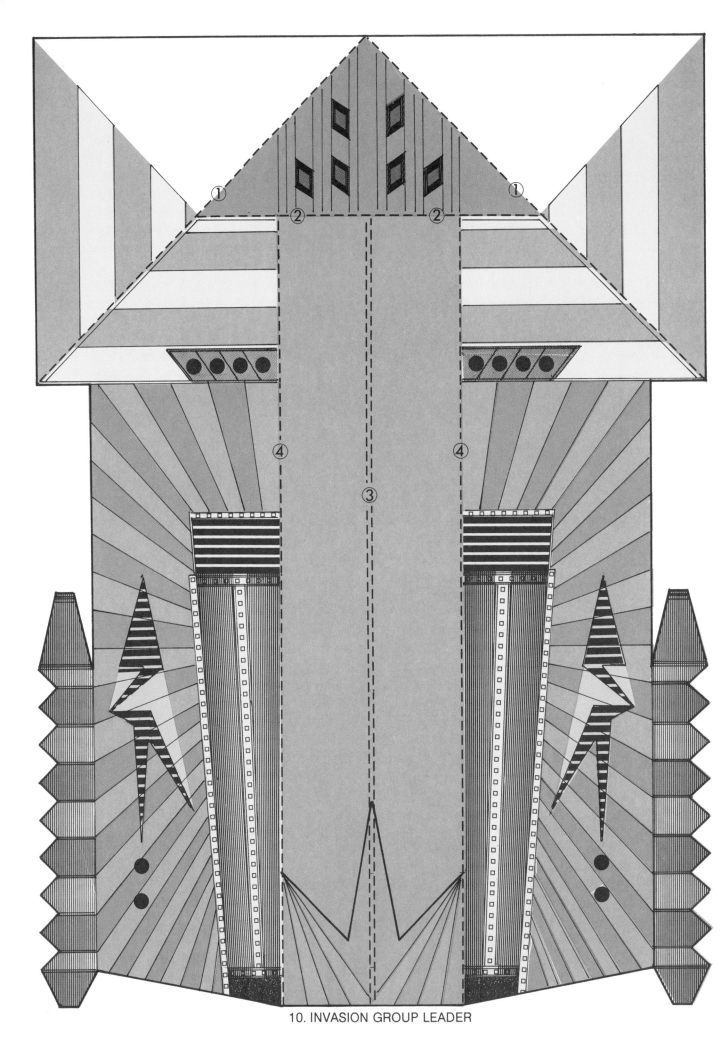

10. INVASION GROUP LEADER

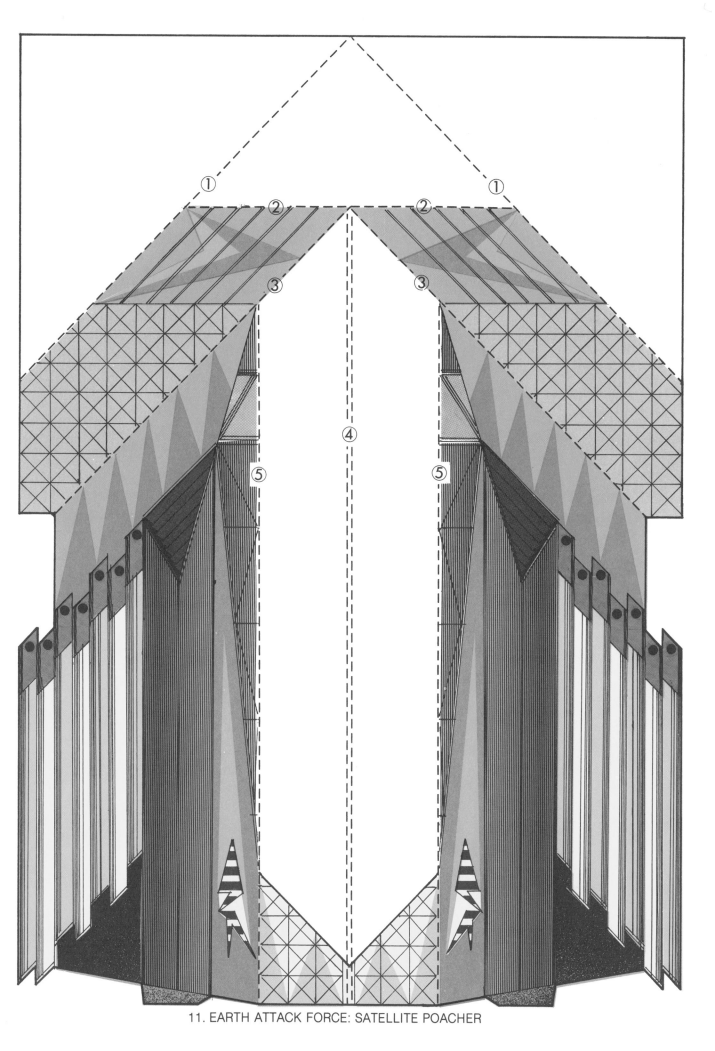

11. EARTH ATTACK FORCE: SATELLITE POACHER

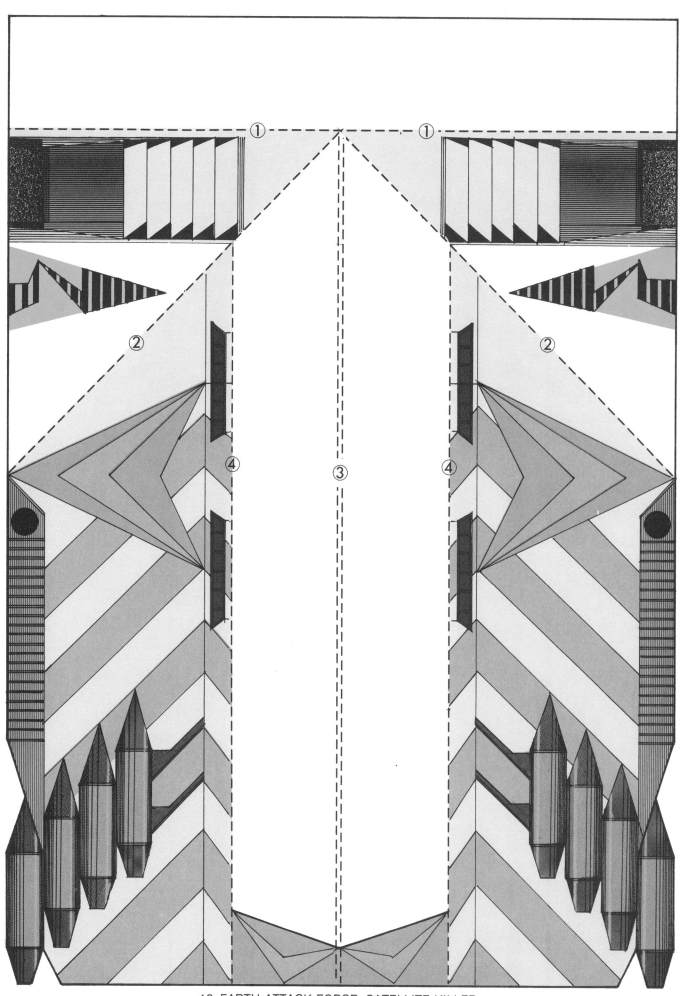

12. EARTH ATTACK FORCE: SATELLITE KILLER

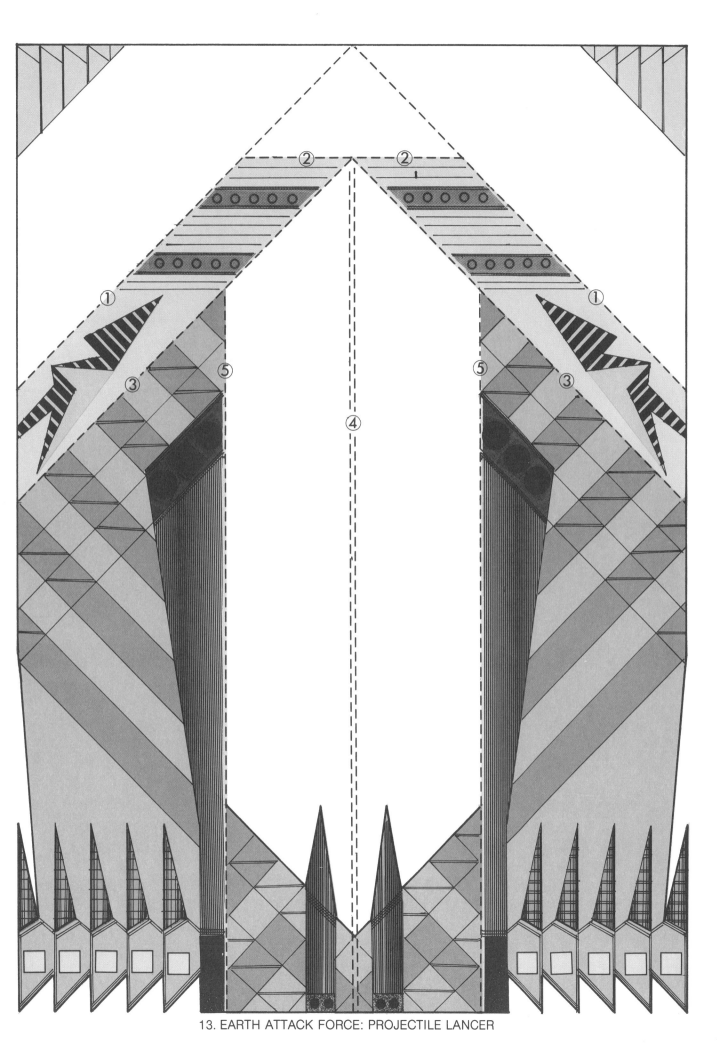

13. EARTH ATTACK FORCE: PROJECTILE LANCER

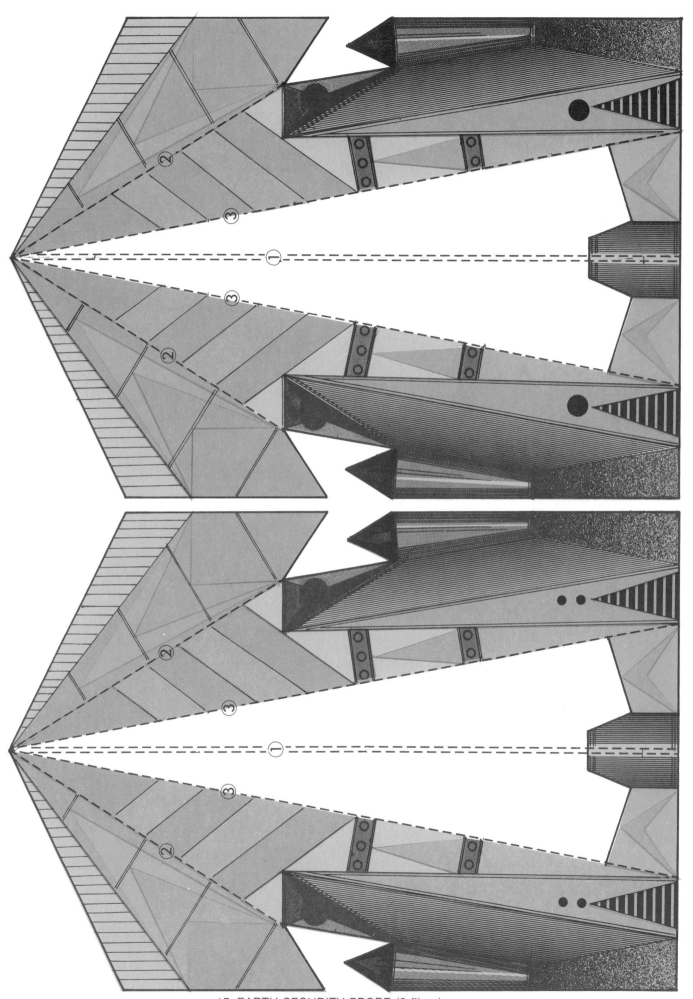

15. EARTH SECURITY PROBE (2 fliers)

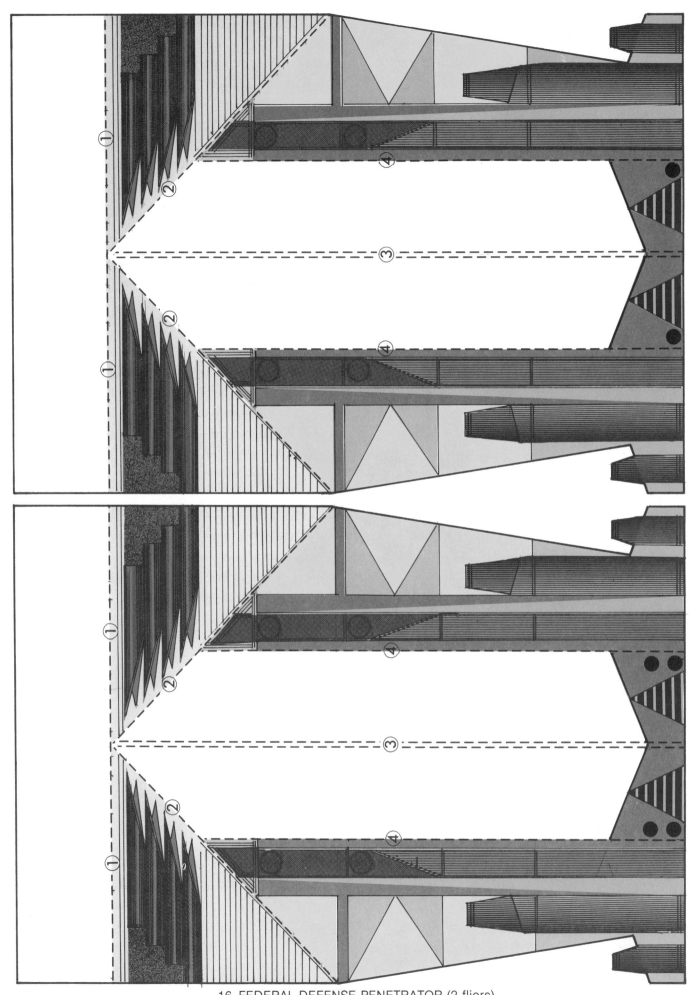

16. FEDERAL DEFENSE PENETRATOR (2 fliers)

EXPLANATORY DIAGRAMS
EARTH DEFENSE FORCE

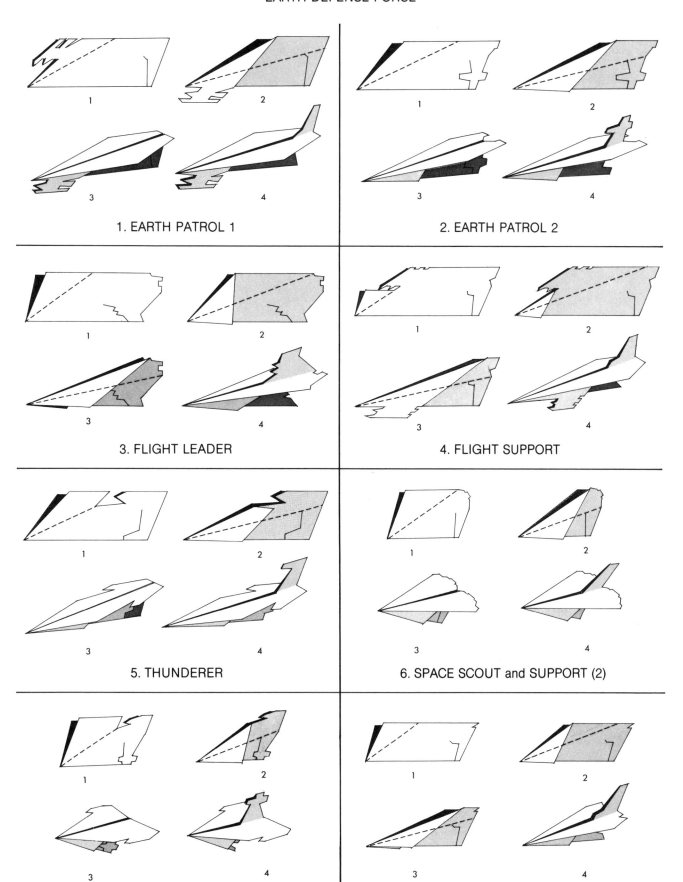

1. EARTH PATROL 1

2. EARTH PATROL 2

3. FLIGHT LEADER

4. FLIGHT SUPPORT

5. THUNDERER

6. SPACE SCOUT and SUPPORT (2)

7. GROUP WING (2)

8. FLIGHT LEADER and SUPPORT (2)

EXTRATERRESTRIAL ATTACK FORCE

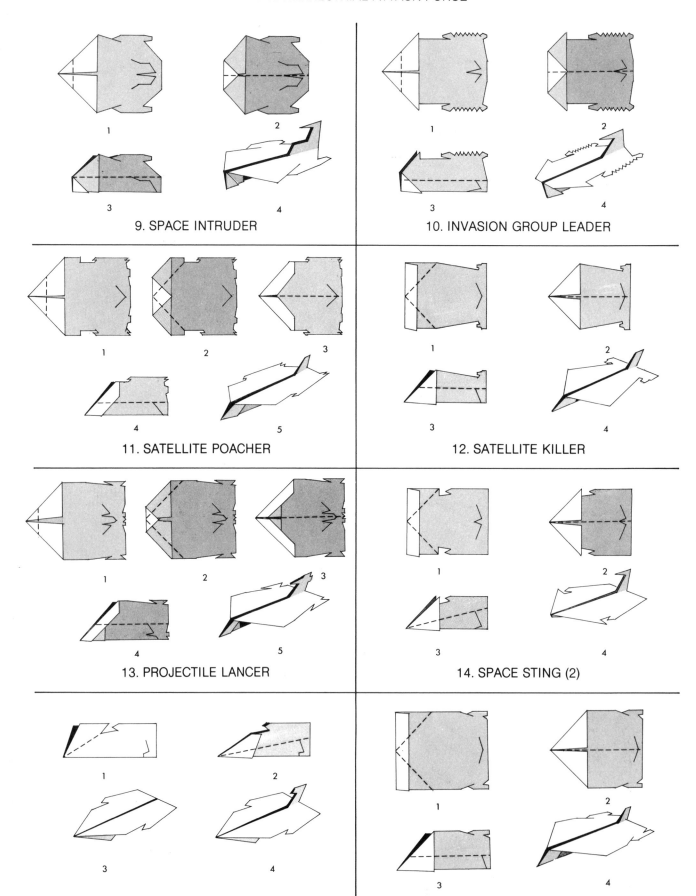

9. SPACE INTRUDER

10. INVASION GROUP LEADER

11. SATELLITE POACHER

12. SATELLITE KILLER

13. PROJECTILE LANCER

14. SPACE STING (2)

15. EARTH SECURITY PROBE (2)

16. FEDERAL DEFENSE PENETRATOR (2)